PORTO

An evening mood on the Rio Douro. The »Barcos Rabelos«, port wine ships, are already in shadow

The Ponte D. Luís caught in the last sunlight. A view over Porto from Vila Nova de Gaia

Arrival in the train station lobby of the »Estação de São Bento«

Azulejo pictures tell of rural life and show scenes from Portuguese history

View from the square in front of the cathedral Sé over the densely-populated district »São Bento da Vitória«

The »Torre dos Clérigos« and the City Hall Tower rise up from the silhouette of the city

Portraits in a side gallery of the »Igreja da Lapa« commemorate the good deeds of these citizens

PORTO

Photos and Text
Werner Radasewsky
Günter Schneider

NICOLAI

Cover photo: Porto's hilly topography
on the Rio Douro

Photo page 10: On the Rio Douro, the two sister cities
Porto and Vila Nova de Gaia lie opposite each other.
There are the »Entrepostos« and the cellarages of the
many port wine companies

Back cover: Traditional port wine ship
»Barco Rabelo« in an Azulejo depiction

© 1989 Nicolaische Verlagsbuchhandlung
Beuermann GmbH, Berlin
All rights reserved

Translation from the German version, »Porto«: Mitch Cohen
Layout: Peter Senftleben
Map: Ingo Naroska
Typesetting: Nagel Fototype, Berlin
Offset Lithography: O.R.T. Kirchner + Graser GmbH, Berlin
Printing and Dust Jacket: Passavia GmbH, Passau
Printed in Germany

ISBN 3-87584-280-4

Ah! I like Porto!
I never lost any sleep
asking why, nor stopped to analyze it.
And if I ever arrived at a conclusion,
it would certainly display
great ignorance – or my fondness

Miguel Torga, *1907
(»Porto«)

Other criteria are applied to port cities than to feudal residences, cultural strongholds, or political centers with their traditional over-zealous desire to impress. Port cities are understated: being supercedes appearance! This is absolutely true for Portugal's second-largest city. It is the only city in the world whose name mirrors this historical role: Porto – port, without any decorative addition to the name, as is the case with so many other »Portos«, »Puertos«, and »Ports« around the globe.

Port cities are sites of international encounters. Here the world meets, and worlds collide with each other. Every port city is a metropolis. Not only wares and goods are exchanged. Every encounter with unfamiliar people has always also brought the experience of different habits, cultures, and convictions – thus there is always the opportunity of testing peaceable contact with persons of varying nationality. Porto can look back over 2000 years of experience in this.

Porto has always been a dynamic and expansive city and has adjusted to the reorientation in international shipping. Maritime activity no longer dominates the immediate appearance of the city. But Porto's centuries-old importance as a national trade metropolis continues, while the city has constantly expanded its international economic connections. The old Portuguese proverb has lost none of its currency: In Lisbon one lives, in Coimbra one studies and in Braga one prays – and in Porto one works and earns the money from which the whole country lives. These days, under the aegis of the Common Market, Porto offers its capacity as a service industry center and is opening its rural surroundings more and more to foreign and domestic manufacturers. Thus the city will remain true to itself by continuing to play an important and expanding role as an economic and industrial region within Europe.

Traditionally, neither the city nor the pragmatic Portoans wear ideological blinders, but rather are open, even if business withdraws behind the dark granite walls – or behind the new concrete walls – into wood-panelled or quite modern offices. Everyday life is all the more turbulent, colorful, and unretouched. In Porto, the city has no cosmetics; no one feels responsible to perform a superficial whitewash.

Cosmopolitan Porto shows itself as it must always have been: unpretentious, businesslike, without any predilection for nostalgia and melodrama, but with a knack for the pleasant sides of life.

It's not only the architecture and the strange metamorphoses that its appearance goes through that spark curiosity, but the friendly and open inhabitants, who make every stay in Porto a pleasant memory.

Werner Radasewsky

PORTO

(VIANA DO CASTELO)
AEROPORTO

LEIXÕES
MATOSINHOS

Estrada da Circunvalação

LINHA DO
MINHO
E DOURO

Rua da
Constituição

Parque
de
Campismo

Parque
da Cidade

Castelo
do Queijo

Praça Marquês
de Pombal

Avenida da Boavista

Praça da
República

FOZ

Museu
e Parque
de Serralves

Rotunda
da
Boavista

Rua do
Almada

Rua de
Sá da Bandeira

(Eléctrico)

Rua de
Santa Catarina

RIO DOURO

OCEANO
ATLÂNTICO

GONDOMAR

AFURADA

(ESPINHO)
(LISBOA)

Ponte
D. Maria Pia

Caves
do Vinho do Porto

VILA NOVA DE GAIA

Trás-os-Montes
e Alto Douro

PORTO

OCEANO
ATLÂNTICO

PORTUGAL

LISBOA

ESPANHA

① Bairro da Sé
② Ribeira
③ Miragaia
④ Fontainhas
⑤ Avenida dos Aliados
⑥ Estação de São Bento
⑦ Torre dos Clérigos
⑧ Palácio da Bolsa
   e Igreja de São Francisco
⑨ Instituto
   do Vinho do Porto

⑩ Solar do Vinho do Porto
   e Museu Romântico
⑪ Palácio
⑫ Museu Nacional
   Soares dos Reis
⑬ Bolhão
⑭ Biblioteca Municipal
⑮ Estação da Trindade
⑯ Templo da Lapa
⑰ Ponte Dom Luís I
⑱ Mosteiro da Serra
   do Pilar

From the airplane, every approach to Porto is beautiful. The core of the city with its wealth of red roofs is recognizable long before the details can be made out. Black arteries run through the chaotic and wide red-brown roofscape, down to the Rio Douro. The buildings in the narrow, interlocking streets throw dark shadows. Porto's skyline is not punctuated by skyscrapers. In the west, the periphery ends abruptly at the Atlantic, which always shimmers with such an intense blue. The mouth of the Rio Douro opens wide at the sea. Three bridges span the broad river, two for cars and one for the railroad. Too few bridgings, as is proven each day anew. These needle's eyes aren't sufficient to prevent nerve-wracking traffic jams.

The beautiful railway bridge is an impressive iron construction. It bears the name of the Queen Dona Maria Pia, but is known the world over as the »Eiffel Bridge«. It was dedicated on November 4, 1877. With it, the French builder Gustave Eiffel had completed his most spectacular construction, after having built numerous other iron constructions – halls and bridges – in Portugal. Not until the Eiffel Tower, dedicated twelve years after Porto's railway bridge, did he exceed it. Gracious and elegant, the »Eiffel Bridge« is no longer adequate to the demands of contemporary times. That's why it was supplemented by a new construction. But, of course, the Ponte Dona Maria Pia remains as a monument symbolizing the architectural *Zeitgeist* of the second half of the last century.

Approaching Porto from the south across the Ponte da Arrábida reveals the fascinating view of a hilly city stretching for many kilometers along the river. Even from a great distance, one sees that it wasn't laid out on a modern drawing board. 2000 years ago, under the name »Portus Cale« – »Calm Port«, the Romans had already made this town into a common expression everywhere in their Empire. Thereafter, the history of the city continues on the same tortuous path as the country's history, greatly influencing it. The name »Portugal« is derived from »Portus Cale«. The »Portus« changed to the city name »Porto«. As a port city, it blossomed into the second largest metropolis in the country, after Lisbon, and today, in the Common Market, it plays the most important economic role for Portugal. A functional metamorphosis has long since been completed.

Formerly a river port, in more recent times Porto has relocated its maritime business to the deep sea port in Leixões to the north, near the international airport. Porto and its greater metropolitan area have developed into a mighty industrial and trade center, economically particularly attractive for investors from all the Common Market countries.

»Cale« was the name of the settlement near the Cathedral Sé, built during the 12th century in the style of a Romanesque fortified church on the foundations of an old Swabian castle. Today, the name of the district »Miragaia«, an ancient quarter with densely crowded little houses, reminds one of the former »Cale«. It is the authentic liveliness and activity of this »Bairro« that is so characteristic and so difficult to capture from outside – that's why it's no use to search for touristic postcards of »Miragaia«. How could postcards showing façades so thoroughly gnawed by the tooth of time convey anything of the spontaneous vitality of the inhabitants?! »Cale« is undergoing its rebirth in the name of the ›New City of Cale‹ in Vila Nova de Gaia, Porto's sister city on the south bank of the Rio Douro. Porto's ›alter ego‹: port wine is associated the world over only with Porto – but all port wine cellarages are to be found in Gaia!

It's so easy to outline and border Porto, to divide it up and sort it into thousands of mosaic tiles, as long as one sticks to dates, epochs, dynasties, and rulers – that is, as long as one carves history up! What a unitary and tremendously enjoyable overall impression one gets of Porto from far away across the river! Even intimate connoisseurs of Porto fall back into the error of thinking of Porto as being well-ordered, completed, tidy, and as digestible as a mature and superb »Vinho do Porto Branco Leve Seco«!

The image offered from above or from afar dissolves more and more as one comes closer to the city: often one is unsuspectedly already in the midst of it, seeking the city's entrances where a map suggests they might be found. The old trade metropolis doesn't seem to be interested in catering to visitors. Finding one's way isn't easy. The access road approaches are labyrinthine, and there are almost no orienting signs to serve as an Ariadne's thread. Of what use are the street names on the map if one seldom finds them on the corners?

The traffic sucks strangers in unmercifully. Thanks to a magical centrifugal force, sooner or later, whether stranger or inhabitant, one is set free again by the metal caravans that strain and agonize their way through the city – and in rare cases suddenly race ahead – and rotated, almost helplessly looking for a way

Early morning: Fish seller in the Rua de Santa Catarina

A chestnut roaster at his smoking vehicle

out, in a circle around the »Rotunda«, one of the main plazas. Be it known: whoever takes the time and goes counterclockwise around this circle with the varying names – »Praça de Mouzinho de Albuquerque«, »Rotunda da Boavista«, or merely (!) the »Rotunda« – is in Porto, if perhaps not at the intended goal of his journey. Grouped around the »Rotunda« are, in order: an S.T.C.P. depot (»Serviço dos Transportes Colectivos do Porto«) with twenty rail entrances, from whose archways »Eléctricos« wait like overgrown carousel vehicles, glancing with their Cyclops faces – in the middle, a single headlight; then, a Baptist church; an immense cemetery (»Cemitério de Agramonte« with white, house-like mausoleums and including a grave decorated with a marble soccer ball); a large market hall; a psychiatric clinic; a labyrinthine six-storey shopping center that includes a movie theater, open daily until midnight; a post office; a gas station; a cabbage field; a railway freightyard; at least 27 ground-level stores from an optician's shop through textiles, groceries, a tunnel-like newsstand, and banks, to antique shops and an auto repair workshop; two stonecutting businesses; about ten cafés and restaurants; a neurologist's practice; additionally: hairdressers, shirtmakers, driving and language schools; streetcar and bus passengers waiting in orderly lines; an indescribable hodgepodge of architectural styles ... No claim is here made to completeness, especially not concerning the diverse puddles in wet or dry seasons, the uncountable small and large building sites and the functionless, fading crosswalk stripes. Only a memory: bullfights, no longer of any importance in Porto, once were staged here.

Noise, confusion, and chaotic traffic without signals or traffic police reigns on the outer traffic lane ring of the »Rotunda«. Eight streets empty into the »Rotunda«; the entire commotion continues in the Rua de Júlio Dinis with its many cafés and shops and, three corners further, in the Avenida da Boavista.

In the plaza's inner ring, where the traffic also ruled once in the past, colorful flower beds have been planted, trees tower upward, a small newsstand waits, weathered wooden benches invite one to take a rest, a few strollers drift by – how are they to keep penetrating the outer traffic ring alive?! It's extremely risky in June, because then a »Feira« opens its gates – a street fair with many small open air restaurants. Then there's also a telephone booth hiding (»Nacional Internacional«) – and, one can't miss it, a high monument in the middle. There,

45 meters up, a lion is drastically and graphically finishing off an eagle. Nights, cascades of spotlights light up everything, including the martial events on the monument's pedestal: horses dying, a cannon being pushed, a »Victória« throwing herself, Amazon-like, against storming troops – an allegorical image of important and influential parts of the city's and Portugal's history. The »Rotunda« – pure Porto!

On the »Monumento à Guerra Peninsular«, the dying eagle symbolizes the Napoleonic troops and the lion stands for the victorious Portuguese-British alliance of those days. Monuments usually commemorate dates, heroic deeds, or persons and seldom are able to depict the complexity of historical processes with their causes and consequences. This monument in the middle of the »Rotunda« can also be compared with the tip of an iceberg: a section of history is presented, but substantially more remains hidden. The British stood at the side of the Portuguese at the beginning of the 19th century. The two nations have the longest and most stable relations of any two European states.

From this first half of the last century, the historical kaleidoscope should be turned back several historical stages. The flashback shows that Portugal is the oldest European nation-state. After centuries of Moorish occupation of the Iberian Peninsula, in the 12th century's »Reconquista«, Dom Afonso Henriques, the later founder of the Portuguese state, was able to drive the Moors out of the area that is Portugal today. The wide area around Porto, however, was really securely in Arab hands for barely 50 years. Portugal was »born« bit by bit from the north to the south. Guimarães, in Porto's neighborhood, is regarded as the »cradle of the nation«: the little city – birthplace of the country's founder – was the first capital. In 1147, Lisbon was »reconquered« with the help of German and French crusaders.

When Dom Afonso Henriques died in 1185, Portugal's borders had nearly reached what they are today. The country has been a sovereign state since 1128, when independence from the royal house of Léon was won in the battle of São Mamede at Guimarães.

Since the end of the 12th century, many Galicians and German Franks settled in Northern Portugal. Their intermingling with the prior population is as visible, even today, as is that of the Moors in the province of Algarve, although the latter were there for so much longer. A leap in time through history shows that Porto had already been wrested from the Moors in 1050, and that the city

The museum »Soares dos Reis«: Dom Afonso Henriques, founder of the Portuguese state, dominates the scene

Not only monuments, churches, and façades testify to Porto's centuries of unbroken history. Beautiful cars from the beginning of the automobile era can be seen more often on Porto's streets than anywhere else in Europe – whether Italian Ansaldos or Bugattis, American Auburns or Buicks, French Ballots or Citroën veterans, British Bentleys, Spanish Hispano-Suiza, or German DKW. Here a 6-cylinder Opel convertible from the year 1933

has steadily developed into a center for trading houses, businessmen, and international economic relations. The trade relationships with Northern Europe, with the cities of the Hanseatic League, with Flanders, and especially with England contributed to the cosmopolitan aura of the city and to its openness toward all kinds of political influences of the various time periods, especially toward liberal influences. Thus it was only fitting that, already in the early Middel Ages, Porto's City Council forbid the nobility to settle in the city. Thus, in Porto today, one finds magnificent houses of the wealthy and impressive trade offices, but no blue-blooded city palaces.

Then, in the 19th century, the city resisted Napoleon's troops vehemently, initially in vain. Napoleon intended to divide Portugal into three parts: the South and the North were to be reigned by various Spanish rulers, with whom the Frenchman had reached an agreement in 1807 in the Contract of Fontainebleau, while the middle and the coastal province of Estremadura were to become French. At the same time, it was planned to divide Brazil and Portugal's colonies between Spain and France. In 1807, General Junot began the plan's execution, occupying Portugal before the latter knew what had happened, and with no resistance worth mentioning. The royal family fled to Brazil.

Through several historical detours, this occupation led to a very far-reaching dispute between two Portuguese kings, who were also brothers: Dom Pedro and Dom Miguel. The first had led Brazil to independence from Portugal, and later claimed the throne in the mother country, which the second did not intend to give up. The brothers' quarrel also embodied the conflict of principles between the last strains of Absolutism and the more liberal Constitutional Monarchy, which Pedro favored. It was a thorny path with many hardships before the Brazilian ex-emperor was enthroned as Dom Pedro IV, and the political and liberal battlefield was Porto. Sieges (1832–1833), hunger, epidemics, civil war were the stages on the way to a monarchy that paved the way for Liberalism in Portugal. Without the support of the citizens of Porto, this path could not have been taken. And England was always an important outpost, sometimes for one, sometimes for the other side. And in the same way, Napoleon's plan of dividing Portugal between France and Spain was also thwarted.

The monument in the middle of the »Rotunda«, begun in 1909 and not finished until 1945, commemorates not only national and international shifts in power, but also, indirectly, in its name »Monumento à Guerra Peninsular«, the often so troubled relationship between the two neighboring Iberian states.

At another and quite hidden spot, the Portoans' long historical memory is intensely exhibited. A small, roofed-over bronze plaque is inlaid in the wall of a building on the »Cais da Ribeira«, near the spot where the Portoans fleeing the Napoleonic troops tried in vain to cross a pontoon bridge to the opposite shore, drowning by the thousands. The bronze plaque depicts this scene. Every day, little bouquets are left here in memory of the event.

Market stalls, vendors, dogs, pigeons, and children dominate the scenery here in the old quarter, »Ribeira«. Music sounds from the »Tascas«. The apparently stamped-down footpath above the waterline is so different from the crumbling cement sidewalks with their waffle pattern: creased, large granite plates exude a medieval appearance. The low parapet shows the traces of iron eyelets and rings, from the days when ships still docked here. Now, people fish here, and a boat for tourist outings rolls at the quay. The stores and production sites in the cave-like walls sometimes seem more like dungeons than businesses. The ground is broken up inside abandoned buildings, and the river can not only be seen between the poles far below, but also smelled.

The »Largo do Terreiro« falls toward the water. The sloping little plaza makes the crowded »Ribeira« more airy, if not for everyone: a traffic sign prohibiting cars shows one in a design of the 1930's. »Tascas« with the swinging doors so typical of Porto, a little reminiscent of the Wild West; a little chapel; heavy candelabras on a gate entrance; and the coat-of-arms of the Consulate of the Netherlands – these are examples of the facets composing not only the »Largo do Terreiro«, but also the »Ribeira« as a whole: dissimilar and nonetheless fitting together. Steps and alleys climb upward.

A few meters further stands the alleged house of Henry the Navigator's birth, today a museum. A half-arc shaped gateway leads through the unadornedly simple façade. A little brass sign reads »Arquivo Histórico (Casa do Infante)«. It is certain that Henry the Navigator – Infante Dom Henrique – was born in 1394 somewhere in the »Ribeira«. His life was marked

In auto junkyards (»Sucatas«), car enthusiasts still find the most unusual pieces for their lovingly maintained and often exotic vehicles. Everything is layered systematically on the walls and hangs in orderly fashion from the ceiling. Antique as well as modern cars are parked in old, often labyrinthine, huge house garages. No other city is so much tunneled under with basement garages

As Emperor of Brazil, Dom Pedro IV first led this former colony to independence from Portugal. The monument also recalls the power struggle between Pedro and his brother Miguel for the Portuguese throne, the collision of contrary political ideas, and, thus, Porto as a city with a long rebellious and liberal past

by a mood of the onset of great things. In 1415, under the leadership of his father Dom João I, Crown Prince Henry, son of Philippa of Lancaster, the only English queen in Portugal, he participated in the occupation of the flowering Arabian trade center Ceuta in North Africa. The Portoans had to sacrifice all their livestock to supply the 8,000-man army that set out in 100 ships to capture Ceuta. Porto's inhabitants were left with the innards – the »Tripas«. And to this day, that's what they proudly call themselves: »Tripeiros«, the tripe-eaters. A Portoan menu without »Tripas« is unimaginable.

With the capture of Ceuta, a new chapter began in the history of Portugal and almost the entire world. Henry, materially and intellectually well-endowed, began to feel the urge to open up the world for Portugal. The Prince never went to sea again, but the navigational school he founded, where the Arabs' nautical know-how was systematically analyzed, taught, and optimized for Portugal's own purposes, earned him the title »the Navigator«. Since the turn of the 15th to the 16th century, the Portuguese, as the first colonial power and the most important sea power of (then) modern times, explored and conquered nearly the entire world. This had consequences over all the centuries right into the present – for good and for evil. In the »Café Ceuta« in the Rua de Ceuta, the guests have other things to discuss over their cup of espresso, called »Cimbalino« only in Porto.

In the »Ribeira«, the pedestrian passageway runs five meters above the market plateau near the shore, past old barber shops in deep chambers, past renovated buildings and entrances with the conspicuous brass knockers and mail slot covers, over tiny bridges, through archways, and past a number of tourist restaurants. A blocky modern fountain on the »Praça da Ribeira« strains the observer's imagination. Small trucks curve around the corner, coming from the turbulent market. This is the heart of the »Ribeira«, with the children playing soccer, the general to-do, the bustle, the sometimes loud disputes, and then again the inertial dozing of the inhabitants. Here, honorable Porto is so old – but its pulse can definitely be felt elsewhere, as well. The alley of catacombs and arcades, Rua dos Canasteiros, is continued in the Rua da Fonte Taurina, with its hidden sterling restaurants, discos, taverns, and warehouses. Castle-like roofed mini-patios unexpectedly open up new views (Nr. 62/64). With their whining vehicles, moped riders buzz-saw through the sonorous stillness of the small, upward-bending Rua de Reboleira, whose wrought iron balconies seem to touch each other. The Travessa do Outeirinho passes under a pedestrian crossover whose beautiful Azulejo decoration and window forms testify to former magnificence, dignity, and importance. Two or three topographical ›storeys‹ higher, still this side of the streetcar stop »Infante«, a huge complex towers up, consisting of the »Igreja de São Francisco« from the 14th and 15th centuries and, architecturally integrated, the noble restaurant of the so magnificent »Palácio da Bolsa«, finished 500 years later and »tongue-and-grooved« into the church's form. All these »fossilized« remains of past epochs are separated by only a few meters, but also by centuries – both the first-time visitor and the old hand lose their feeling for time.

In the entire »Baixa«, or downtown area, shop is lined up next to shop in the buildings staggered like steps in the streets leading upward and down: from the »Mercearia«, a fruit store in front and shoe repair shop in the back, from the endless textile stores through cafés, pastelarias, and confeitarias to the »Frangos para vender à angolana« grills, where chickens are prepared the way the Portuguese learned in their former colony, Angola: spicy and barbecued over charcoal. In the long Rua do Almada, the specialty shops make way for each other every few steps, as they also do in the Rua de Sá da Bandeira or in the exquisite Rua de Santa Catarina, which, from the busy »Praça da Batalha« on, has been rebuilt as a pedestrian street, in essence. The Rua de Cedofeita invites one to stroll as does the so-called Rua Escura, the ›dark street‹ in both the literal and the metaphorical sense.

Heavy and often gloomy granite façades are enlivened by houses built of red and green clinker blocks, by many small Azulejo decorations, and by countless wrought iron adornments and balconies. There, where Porto shows itself most massively, one need only open a door: for example in the crowded, loud Rua Formosa 216 or 234; there passageways lead, as if into a village, into the »Quintais«, tube-like courtyard gardens so characteristic of Porto, with crowing roosters, orange trees, and vegetable beds.

Porto seems all the more disparate, the more it presents itself as a city, and all the more homogeneous, the more it is a village. A general Portuguese antagonism!

Porto is wild, disordered and confused, sometimes bursting and crumbling, and there is something oriental

Portus Cale – peaceful harbor – was the name the Romans gave to this settlement on the river. The times have polished down the language until the name Portugal emerged. ›Porto‹ remained as the name for the harbor city on the Rio Douro – the fundamental reorientation of European seafaring is bound up with it. The birth house of Henry the Navigator is still on the »Ribeira«. He founded a school for ship's captains whose graduates started a whole chapter of world history with their voyages of discovery in the name of trade, the Church, and the King. – The »Marégrafo«, the continent's oldest – and still functioning – water-level gauge is installed in a small house at the mouth of the Rio Douro

*The man with the large hat: Infante Dom Henrique -
Henry the Navigator, the city's best known native son.
A wood sculpture in the »Palácio da Bolsa«*

*Regularly making headlines in the world of sports:
the »Futebol Clube do Porto«*

in its bustle. And, at the same time, this ancient European trade city finds its identity in its hidden and so elegant interior life, in its understated and markedly friendly people, in the ambience somewhat influenced by the historical contact with the cities of the Hanseatic League, where the dignified reserve of the trading houses hides from a city overflowing with tumult.

In the large area around the »Praça dos Leões«, where a fountain splashes under high palms, cars park illegally and everything is a confusion of streets looking like squares and plazas crossed by through-traffic from all directions. Passers-by hurry out from the end station of the »Eléctrico« in all directions. Many of them are students on the way to the main gate of the University, or to one of the student cafés. It swarms here; and exactly here is where everything was once so systematically planned and built.

The 15th and 16th centuries had shown interest solely in trade; but this led to such a large stockpile of money in the state treasury that, in the 17th century, several major representative constructions were erected in the »Porto Baroque« style (for example, the churches São Bento, Carmo, Misericórdia, as well as the »Torre dos Clérigos«). As the 18th century neared its end, first João de Almada (died 1786), and then his son Francisco (1757–1804) went to work.

At that time, the Marquês de Pombal, Portugal's most versatile and charismatic politician of all times, held the political scepter in his hand. A Rationalist, he was a true manifestation of the European Enlightenment. The Almadas were the Marquês' intimates and relatives. Just as he had shouldered the task of rebuilding Lisbon after it was destroyed by the earthquake in 1755 – a modern and revolutionary plan for the conditions of those days –, these »urbanizadores« wanted to revamp Porto. Many constructions still in existence today go back to the father: the »Feitoria Inglesa« – the English trade house – and also the huge »Hospital de Santo António«, which spreads out just a few steps down from the »Praça dos Leões«. The building was never completed – it was supposed to be an architectural pendant to the mighty cloister convent of Mafra, north of Lisbon. But not only the dimensions of Porto's largest hospital are impressive. When Almada Jr. died at the age of 47, Porto's city-planning clearly bore his signature.

Porto is no city for bicyclists, and not just because of the bumpy cobblestones that sometimes seem to date back to Francisco de Almada's time.

Just a little further down – where the »Torres dos Clérigos« can no longer be seen – the aged terrace of a Miradouro sprawls on the Passeio das Virtudes, exhibiting a
view over the Rio Douro. Suddenly stillness reigns, punctuated only by the mixed voices of children playing. The
Rua das Virtudes curves over hunched streets, past a
very old fountain embedded in the wall of a building
(Nr. 1), then blending into the Rua da Horta, a street so narrow it's nearly invisible, reminiscent of a medieval village
alley. This opens up unexpectedly onto something like a
castle's rampart with a wide view over the city: red-
brown roofs with their »Clara Bóias«, the Sé Cathedral in
the distance, the Ponte D. Luís I, and Vila Nova de Gaia.
One sees everyday life, hears and smells it. Sloping up,
sloping down – and soon one lands at the Rua dos Caldei-
reiros with its weird-seeming orthopedic and artificial
limb businesses. Descending it in a narrow arc, one
reaches the Rua das Flores, the city's former center for
exquisite jewelry, with exclusive shops even today: then,
lower, the Rua de Ferreira Borges. The all-important and
imposing Port Wine Institute is located here, as is the
impressive bourse and, prized by artlovers, the »Mercado Ferreira Borges«, a former market hall, beautifully
restored and with changing exhibits – all brought together in a harmonious metropolitan ensemble. In front
of them, on a white pedestal, a monument of Henry the
Navigator stands, one finger pointing the way across the
street named for him, the Rua do Infante D. Henrique, to
the Atlantic in the west. The house where he is supposed
to have been born is a stone's throw from here.

Infante is the name of the end station of the »Eléctrico«,
directly on the shore street. The streetcar runs beside
the Atlantic as far as the northern industrial suburb
Matosinhos. Do the city fathers regret sacrificing so
many »Eléctrico« lines to the automobile in recent years?
The sky is still full of wires, for some of the »Eléctricos«
have been replaced with electrically-powered double-
decker trolleys. Children hang onto the outsides of the
two- or four-axled »Eléctricos«. »Construido nas Oficinas
da Comp. a Carris de Ferro do Porto 1928« reads a sign in
a wood-panelled »Eléctrico« with its cast iron-framed
seats – a row with seats in pairs, the other for singles. A
lot of sliding glass in the interior – the »guillotine windows« are moved vertically – and one leans one's elbows
comfortably on an armrest at the usually open window,
pulling on the bell-rope when it's time to get off.

*Hard contrasts: In the crowded construction of the
inner city, the centuries appear to be piled up, stone on
stone. At the same time, a generous construction style
emerged, clearly visible in the angular villas with their
many pergolas. To the north and south of the Avenida da
Boavista, individual city districts with tree-lined
boulevards are laid out spaciously. The Social Housing
Projects, built decades ago, are still models for emulation.
Here a characteristic town house in the area of the Avenida
dos Combatentes da Grande Guerra*

*Azulejo decoration is found throughout the entire city –
to an even greater extent than elsewhere in Portugal.
As large-format depictions on private buildings, or on
churches in the form of huge blue-and-white façade
decoration with sacred motifs – and almost everywhere
the dark granite façades are beautified by delicate, pastel-
colored tile decoration or by tender Art Nouveau
ornaments*

The ride goes past »Miragaia«, where the street wends its
way like a levee, along past the sunken old two- and
three-storey buildings, so slender and hung with drying
laundry. The »Eléctrico« stops at short intervals, usually
at the height of the second storey, the electric motor
softly burbling.

In the old »Miragaia«, the stores sit deeper than the
street in low arcade passages. Variously and complicat-
edly »stacked up«, the buildings trail up the hill. Steps like
the »Escadas do Recanto« penetrate into this old district.
Beforehand, one passes the dock facilities, old wooden
warehouses, and a freightyard situated in front of them
on the river, whose rails – abracadabra – suddenly disappear through a tunnel into the belly of the city; then
one also passes »Alfândega«, the former main customs
office with the outstretched bars of cranes.

One's glance sweeps over the river to Vila Nova de
Gaia, to the steeply ascending viaduct of the Rua General
Torres, and to the »Barcos Rabelos«, which make a pretty
picture in front of the advertisements for all the port
wine cellarages. Again and again, warehouses like the
»Companhia Arrozeira Mercantil« recall Porto's former
importance as a river port. The riverbank seems to
approach within arm's distance during the ride, as do the
small wooden boats, the flower beds, factories, the little
building with the old »Marégrafo« tide recorder. A ferry
steers toward the fishing village Afurada, which stretches along the opposite shore of the river's mouth.

There, laundry waves unceasingly on the lines between the high, x-shaped poles, there the fishing nets are
piled up, there the cutters are hauled ashore. With their
typical sash-like scarves thrown over their shoulders,
the women scrub their laundry at the central washing
place as they have for ages – sometimes singing together, sometimes laughing loudly, and occasionally
scolding at the top of their lungs. Old men indulge in idle-
ness and village gossip. Here, the metropolis Porto is
present only as a backdrop of sound from the opposite
shore – and seems to be very, very far away.

Passing the palms standing at the »Jardim do Passeio
Alegre« with its two entrance obelisks, fountains, and the
»Chalet«, the »Eléctrico« then wobbles further through
the narrow curves, bending off at »Foz«, grinding its sing-
ing-scratching way with more speed along the seashore
on the Avenida do Brasil, past the esplanades and view-
ing terraces, past the beach and the palm promenades.
»Foz« at the ocean and – higher up in the hills – »Foz
Velha« are among the privileged residential areas, even if

the village character has held out in this region. There are still architectural witnesses to times gone by, with plenty of Sleeping Beauty green, as in the Rua Alto de Vila: heavy granite walls that never deteriorate, and behind which no one has lived for a long, long time.

Even from a distance, the equestrian stature of D. João VI is conspicuous in front of the remains of a wrecked tanker on the wide space of the »Praça de Gonçalves Zarco« at the so-called »Cheese Castle«. The »Forte S. Francisco Xavier« (1661–1662) is one of three bastions in »Foz«; the King gazes at an angle over his horse toward the southwest and Brazil, where he was Emperor almost 200 years ago. He was also the father of the two enemy brothers Miguel and Pedro, who influenced the history of Portugal and Porto so enduringly.

Straight as an arrow, the kilometer-long Avenida da Boavista connects this square with the downtown »Rotunda« and its historical monument recalling the Spanish-French-Portuguese conflicts. The »Boavista« is also travelled by an »Eléctrico« line. From the Rua das Campinas, which meets the »Boavista«, the atmosphere changes: behind one is the city, the old, dignified houses of the wealthy amid large gardens containing a great variety of species, that retreat little by little before shopping centers and hotels; and, south of the wide »Boavista«, the quiet, tree-lined, beautiful streets near the Rua do Campo Alegre and the so wonderfully green islands like the »Instituto Botânico Dr. Gonçalo Sampaio«, or the »Faculdade de Letras«, a University institute. And, looking to the west, the »Boavista« slopes down one more time; suddenly the broad horizon emerges, and the ocean and, to the right, woods, fields, and horses show themselves.

Further down, the »Eléctricos« ride alongside the ocean as far as Matosinhos, an unusual mixture of beach, factories, and port area, which makes itself noticeable with all sorts of smells, and where several excellent »Marisco« and fish restaurants wait unexpectedly. Matosinhos and Espinho – these are Porto's two outposts on the ocean, the one in the north, and the other in the south with the colorful bustle one expects of sea resorts. Both little cities' streets are laid out strictly in right-angles, something unknown in Porto's »Baixa«; and in Espinho the streets are numbered – parallel to the ocean, even; perpendicular, odd.

The »Eléctrico« rails end abruptly in the pavement of Matosinhos; driver and conductor switch the tap-bow on the wire above, the seats are unfolded in the opposite

The North African Moors brought along the »Al-Zulaich« – the ›gleaming stone‹ – to the Iberian Peninsula, which they occupied for centuries until their expulsion (»Reconquista«) by Afonso Henriques. In the Azulejo, a cultural heritage lives on. – Here the suburban train station »Granja«. The station official poses in front of an Azulejo picture of the National Monument »Batalha«, heavy with history

direction, and the destination-sign is turned to Porto – after Carmo, Foz, Rotunda, Boavista, or Infante.

The Rio Douro has long been chosen as the training ground for canoeists and paddlers, who have their docking points on the other side of the »Eiffel Bridge« on the green shores of Vila Nova de Gaia. One watches them and has, at the same time, impressive glances into everyday life in Porto from the nearly hidden Rua do Sol, with its high trees, old pavement, and little houses crowding around this »Miradouro«. From here one can go directly into the bustling »Fontainhas« district, which spreads out in the neighborhood of the Rua de Gomes Freire like terraces overlooking the Rio Douro.

Here is where Porto's city festival, St. John's Night, from June 23 to June 24, is celebrated with the most merriment. This district's liveliness is so very much in contrast to the peacefulness of the nearby »Cemitério do Prado do Repouso«. The countless workshops in the Rua do Duque de Saldanha bordering the cemetery are filled with indefatigable activity. Only a passageway interrupts this strange bustle, leading into an old residential quarter preserved as an architectural monument. Here, ancient little houses and apartment buildings from the beginning of this century complement each other wonderfully in quiet isolation. Another wall separates the cemetery from the open grounds of the military museum; cannon barrels tower here, crosses for the dead stand there.

Elsewhere, celebration goes on day and night during the warm part of the year. The »Palácio« stands on the crown of a hill, in the middle of a small amusement park with its loud carnival noises and embedded in beautiful natural surroundings that evidence the forming hand of the gardener. In 1865, a fantastic iron and glass construction was erected on this spot, the »Palácio de Cristal«. The name »Palácio« is now synonymous with the »Feira Popular« and its countless small and large open air restaurants with a wide, unencumbered panorama – a meeting place for young and old during the summer. But the crystal palace has been torn down and replaced by a sober concrete dome construction. And the »monkey village« no longer exists, either; sometimes chimpanzees, half-wild, are still seen performing acrobatics through the branches.

Below the »Palácio«, in the Rua de Entre de Quintas with its many cats, one plunges unexpectedly into a quiet evergreen idyll. The pretty little »Museu Romântico« has moved into the building of the former »Quinta da Macieirinha« and shows how people used to live in Porto. Below it, the »Solar do Vinho do Porto« opens its doors. There, in the very cultivated atmosphere of this elegant ›branch office‹ of the »Instituto do Vinho do Porto«, one can enjoy the various port wines, which are decanted in the authentic style, in »Cálices«. The glance wanders over the well-kept gardens, where even grapefruits tree grow, and along the shores of the river to the activity in the alleys around the Rua da Viela do Picoto, which seems so medieval. There a »Quinta« is hidden behind stout walls, an old presence surrounded by lush nature, of which there is so much in Porto but which nonetheless seems so often to evade one's sight. Up here the green dome of the »Palácio« glows through the trees like a flying saucer that has just landed.

One even finds grapes growing on the »Ramadas«, the wine pergolas so typical for Northern Portugal. Beside the lush, colorful camellias, the vines twine over the short walls that line the crooked alleys up to the »Largo de Santa Catarina«. Surrounding the little plaza and the small chapel is a stone parapet whose whitewash has long since faded and peeled.

A romantic spot, seemingly far away from the doings of the Big City down there on the shore street, Rua do Ouro. One gazes entranced at the mouth of the river and its golden shimmering sandbank, and finds oneself at the end of an imaginary axis that crosses the Ponte da Arrábida and unites with the viewpoint-terrace of the »Solar do Vinho do Porto«.

Within the field of view of both »Miradouros« lies Vila Nova de Gaia, Porto's port wine city on the other side.

There the ground slopes up steeply from the shore street Avenida Diogo Leite. Hiding behind high walls of field stones are the huge »Entrepostos«, the stone warehouses of the port wine firms. It smells like »Vinho Fino«. That is the name true Portoans – the »Tripeiros« – give their wine, which is already enriched with brandy before its long journey from the winegrowing regions of the Alto Douro. On the other walls of the cellarages, so near the shore, the water levels are still marked from the days when the Rio Douro annually overflowed. Now the danger of high water has been controlled by newly-constructed dams. Vila Nova de Gaia has two faces: to accommodate the traffic heading to or from Porto, the city's layout has been changed, including the alignment of the new railway bridge, which replaces the Ponte D. Maria Pia. The pretty »Museu Terxeira Lopes« is very difficult to find. The production of port wine in the traditional »Armazens« has remained, securing jobs for many inhabitants.

Past the cellerages with their long, pointed roofs, past a customs house on the river, past cranes at a small shipbuilding yard, a long road leads beside the Rio Douro; and on the other shore, below the »Palácio«, one sees the »Eléctrico« struggling up the steep Rua da Restauração. The stretch on the quay »Capelo Ivens« turns into an expedition into the fossilized past of Porto and Vila Nova de Gaia. The old warehouses and depots, some standing empty, some still functioning, call up associations of the times when sailing ships, steamers, and the freighters of the merchant marine from far and near docked on the quays of this river. Today, there are only anglers. Gate entrances lead to once lordly and now abandoned mansions, in whose gardens an oil refinery has been installed. The elevators in the 80 meter high bridge piers of the Ponte da Arrábida no longer fulfill their purpose. The inhabitants of the fishing village Afurada reach the other, the Porto shore of the Rio Douro on the little ferry as they have always done. The »Eléctricos« that connect the outer districts on the ocean with the »Baixa«, downtown, stop at the dock.

At the seam of the Avenida de Montevideu and the Avenida do Brasil, terraces and promenades, gardens and beach cafés spread out in two compass directions along the Atlantic

Dusk may spread over Porto. Then a golden gleam lies on the river, falls increasingly on the roofs, and trickles into the streets. In this show of colors, the truly beautiful face of this seemingly porous city shows itself. For centuries, it has defended itself vehemently against any kind of cosmetics and yet (or certainly: thus) it unfolds its charm every evening! A city whose inhabitants are aware of their unbendingness and who long ago earned it a name as an invincible metropolis – which they will justifiably continue to bear in coming times:

»Porto – Cidade Invicta«

The steep shopping street
Rua de Santo António –
actually the Rua 31 de
Janeiro – is bordered by
churches, broadly clothed
with Azulejos: above, by
the Igreja Santo Ildefonso,
and below, by the Igreja
dos Congregados

Downtown, in the »Baixa«, the broad entrance hall of the
»Estação de São Bento« yawns. The train station at the
head end of a long tunnel was opened in 1916. The huge
dimensions, the opulent Azulejo panels, the inlaid Azulejo
frieze recounting the development from the wheel to the
railway, and the steady stream of travellers create the
impression that this is the main train station. But the main
station is on the eastern periphery and is, architectonically,
no competition for the »Estação de São Bento«

29

The square in front of the »Estação de São Bento« seems to
lie in a valley. The streets rise up in all directions, almost
immediately going downward again. Traffic in the narrow
alleys and streets can be very chaotic. The confusion of
neon advertisements belongs to the city's appearance as do
the inevitable little wrought iron balconies and the
extremely varied wooden frames of the large windows

30

Porto spreads across many hills. The abrupt changes in height up from the river bank run to 60, 80, and 100 meters. The view over the Igreja dos Congregados follows the Avenida D. Afonso Henriques, which lies lower, and the Avenida de Vímara Peres, named for the city's founder. The City Hall Tower and the newspaper building »Jornal de Notícias« stand out on the skyline

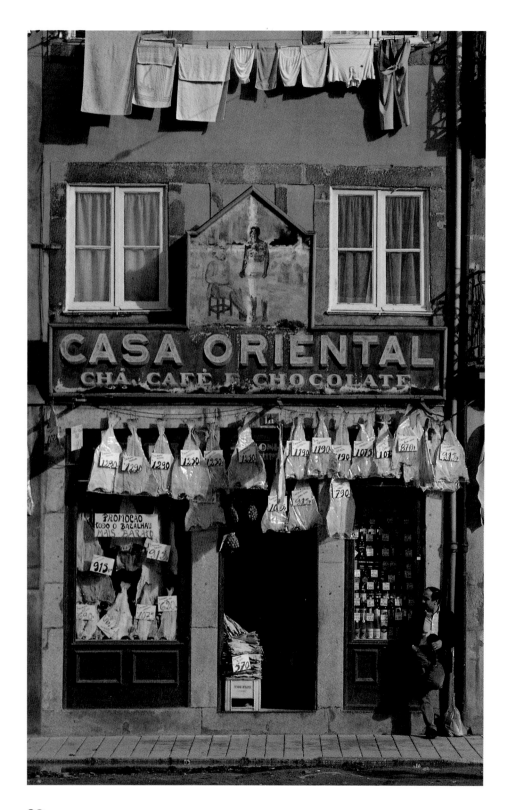

*Innumerable shops, rich in
tradition, also contribute to Porto's
uniqueness. The number one
national dish is prepared from
»Bacalhau« in manifold variations –
stockfish is available everywhere,
not just in the »Casa Oriental«*

*Porto knows no department stores.
The »Casa Pereira« in the Rua de Sá
da Bandeira is one of the many
specialty shops. Here, all sorts of
hunting and fishing articles are
sold. The shops are also impressive
for the artistic carpentry of the
window frames*

The »Casa Hortícola« in the complex of the market hall
»Bolhão« offers every kind of seeds. The business, founded
in 1922, had been a German sausage shop. The walls,
gleaming like marble, are made of fine wood, onto which
the shimmering marble hatching was artistically applied

For about 100 years, no changes have been made in the interior decoration of the »Casa Margaridense« in the Travessa de Cedofeita. The »Pão de Ló« cake, resembling a wagon wheel and especially popular at Easter time, is produced in this family business according to an old recipe – as are the jellies and the marmelade, sold in old porcelain tureens that must be returned

Visual variety is constantly supplied by store window displays: An advertisement for fresh coffee in the Rua de Costa Cabral

Trade in religious articles in the Rua das Flores, where unusual old hardware stores can be found and where the jewelry shops have long concentrated

In the characteristic »Mercearias Finas«, almost everything can be had, from groceries to dry goods. The beautiful wood frame of »A Pérola do Bolhão« in the Rua Formosa is no exception in the cityscape

38

Again and again, Azulejo façades are the faces of the stores, inside and out. In the »Pérola da Guiné«, besides tea (»Chá«), coffee – always freshly roasted – is also sold and ground in the silver grinders

In the central shopping area, under open skies and in
the middle of the »Baixa«, the first floor of the original
»Mercado do Bolhão« is sunk below the level of the street.
The sound of heavy traffic outside does not penetrate up
into the many little shops in the galleries that line the
inside. Despite newer and more accessible market halls,
the »Mercado do Bolhão« has retained its central
importance. Awnings, umbrellas, and plastic sheeting
protect the wares, the vendors, and the customers
from sun – and rain!

40

Flower and vegetable vendor in the »Bolhão«

The vending stands are faced with slate. All products come from the big city's surrounding area

Somewhat south of Porto is Espinho. Every Monday the sea resort, once so rich in tradition, puts on a different face and turns into an open air market. With its enormous bounty of fruit, vegetables, meat, and other foods, of textiles, carpets, household wares, and handicrafts, the »Feira de Espinho« is one of Portugal's most important street markets

Like the still life in a painting – the poultry market on the »Feira de Espinho«: live geese, ducks, turkeys, chickens, pheasants. – Two smaller but equally popular street markets are held Saturdays north of Porto in Senhora da Hora and in Custóias. There, Gypsies offer inexpensive clothing from nearby textile factories whose wares are otherwise found almost exclusively in boutiques and renowned clothing stores throughout Europe

44

The daily market activity and bustle extend into the inner city – with numerous shops on wheels: vendors selling balloons, tin toys, and lottery tickets loudly hawk Kitsch, consumer goods, and candy. On the Praça da Liberdade, shoeshine stands offer their services. In the football newspaper, the latest information is traded

45

Impressive buildings line the broad Avenida dos Aliados.
Since its completion in 1917, banks and law firms, trading
company administrations and the branch offices of
foreign companies have taken up residence here. The cafés
are always full. The traffic lanes are separated by lushly
planted strolling paths. The »Paços do Concelho« – City
Hall – border the square-like street on its north side. The
Avenida dos Aliados slopes downward to the south, where,
on the Praça da Liberdade, the tall equestrian sculpture of
Dom Pedro IV triggers associations of Portuguese history

46

The wooded terrace in front of the »Mosteiro e Convento da Serra do Pilar« is probably the best-known »Miradouro« – which means »viewpoint«. The broadly spread building of this former cloister complex is today primarily used as a barracks. Located on the crown of a hill high above the Rio Douro, the widely visible »Convento« still can not really be considered one of Porto's landmarks. The two traffic levels of the Ponte D.Luís I lead out of Porto and open up into the sister city, Vila Nova de Gaia, below this construction

The »Feitoria Inglesa« from the year 1790 is hidden behind
dark granite walls. It is the only remaining British factory
house of the many that used to stand everywhere
throughout the world. British port wine companies came
and still come together here. As early as 1660, traders,
shipping companies, and port wine producers met here in
what is now the Rua Infante D.Henrique, in the building
that preceded the factory, to talk business. The »Feitoria
Inglesa« looks back over as much unbroken history as the
old, almost never problematical alliance between Great
Britain and Portugal

In the Rua 31 de Janeiro, known as the Rua de Santo António among the residents: Like this one, many old, long-established jewelry shops continue to offer their gold and silver creations. These precious metals are worked into »Filigrana«, finely perforated gilded silver jewelry, whose degree of purity is among the world's highest. The center of the gold and silver smithing is the suburb Gondomar, whose outer features exhibit a hard contrast with the beautiful jewelry produced there

The entrance area of the club-like association »Ateneu
Comercial do Porto«, an outwardly reserved building

In the lowest storey several distinctive billiard salons
are available for members

Interrupted only by the rustle of national and international
newspapers, profound stillness reigns in the reading
room of the »Ateneu Comercial do Porto«. This facility,
one among several of its sort, has existed since 1869.
Aside from the relaxation and exchange of thought that
such »clubs« offer their guests, cultural activities are also
promoted. The members regard themselves as patrons
and don't want their names made public

52

The circle of club members, which includes women,
consists of businesspeople from the established trade
firms. At almost all levels of society, Porto's bustle
and the city's outward reserve are contradicted by the
quiet, distinguished inner life in stylish surroundings.
Restaurants, libraries, and archives – in the »Ateneu«, with
an original script of Camõe's »Os Lusíades« (»The Lusiads«)–,
the barber, and reception rooms round out the picture of
this interior, so atypical of Portugal and so typical of Porto

53

The legendary Belle-Epoque »Hotel Infante Sagres« has
a quite inconspicuous façade, but inside it unfolds its
honorable charm. Scenes from the life of Henry the
Navigator are depicted on the huge wooden panels in the
restaurant. Here in the city of his birth, Infante D.Henrique,
to whom the navigational school in Sagres on the Algarve
coast is attributed, prepared himself for his explorations
of the oceans and sea routes

54

*The »Cimbalino« is served with agility in one of the
countless cafés. Over the small black espresso, the
Portoans – the »Tripeiros« – come to themselves at least
once a day, reading the newspaper and discussing the
news, like here in the »Café Majestic« in the Rua de Santa
Catarina*

The cafés exhibit great variety. Below the Art Deco stained glass artwork with the chic automobile motif, the little restaurant opens its doors. Since 1933, many strollers have regarded the »Pastelaria Confeitaria Arcádia« on the Praça da Liberdade as a meeting place for the small afternoon »lanches« (lunch or snack) and also for tea. Not only is espresso highly honored, Porto also looks back over a long tea (»Chá«) tradition, similar to the English five o'clock tea time

Hours of study, often over a single bottle of mineral water, at the tables of the student café »Aviz« in the Rua Avis with its great variety of bookstores. The waiters are understanding, especially in the wet, cold winter, when the apartments in the old buildings with their granite walls refuse to get dry and warm. »In tremendis tauradis/ cum Prof. Azarisque/viximus tinto cum vino/pinguis cafae Avisque« is one of the slogans – in Latin, in this case. In grateful remembrance of the many hours in the »Aviz«, university graduates have left what rhymes and what has no rhyme nor reason on small plaques affixed to the walls

In the form of a question mark, the Rio Douro empties in
the west into the Atlantic after its 640 kilomters journey.
Humans had settled here even in prehistoric times. From
the Roman Portus Cale derive not only ›Portugal‹ but also
›Gaia‹. This is the name borne by Porto's »new« sister city –
Vila Nova de Gaia – across the river, on the south bank.
But the actual Cale was located in the area of today's
Porto. The upper traffic level of the Ponte D.Luís I is one of
the four bridgeheads between Porto and the port wine city
Vila Nova de Gaia

Every year, in the night from the 23rd to the 24th of June,
the festival in honor of São João is celebrated. Across the
Rio Douro one sees the Fontainhas district, where this
festival is celebrated under the open sky in its authentic,
unbounded form – not without some glasses of »Vinho
Fino«, as the Portoans call port wine. Now people come
who otherwise seldom find their way into this area.
St.John's Night begins at moonrise and ends at dawn.
People beat each other symbolically with squeaking plastic
hammers and long stalks of leek – happily believing in the
magical powers of this summer night

59

The roof landscape of the port wine cellarage in Vila Nova de Gaia. In the »Entrepostos« (cellarages), the various kinds of port wine mature until bottling: The taste and color palette of the »Vinho do Porto« stretches from very dry and nearly glass-clear white, to very smooth and deep red. The port wine reaches the national and international market only after many years, sometimes even decades. The grapevines are not cultivated in Porto

One of the internationally known port wine producers lets the wine, still young, age about a year in the largest barrels in the world. The 120 »Balseiros« contain 60.000 liters each and are to be found far to the east of Porto near Peso da Régua in the province Trás-os-Montes e Alto Douro. A worker in the state »Casa do Douro« determines the quality of the wines. The port wine manufacturers deliver samples of all harvests of a year. In this »Tunel«, a large wine barrel, the »Casa do Douro« also stores its rarities

61

RIO DOURO
PINHÃO

Timelessly beautiful, Azulejos report the stations of the grape harvest. North and south of the Rio Douro, between Régua and the Spanish border to the east, the vineyard terraces spread over four districts and about 170 localities. Grape growing is an important factor for the general economy as well as for the job market. If the »Vindimas«, grape-harvest time, is always accompanied by many village festivals, the hard work in the hot vineyards has nothing to do with folklore – even less in olden days than now. The »Pipas«, the barrels, were brought to the river banks on oxcarts and loaded there onto the characteristic »Barcos Rabelos«. The port wine ships sailed westward along the sometimes treacherous river to Porto. In the meantime, tanker trucks have adopted this task. Today the »Barcos Rabelos« are a decorative backdrop

The highly technologized
port wine production is
unthinkable without the
»Vindimadores«, the
pickers with their typical
baskets

*»Quintas« are old land
houses in the middle of
large vineyards, some of
which have joined the
»Turismo de Habitação«,
housing travellers
within their noble walls*

65

One of the leading port wine companies calls this strictly controlled wine cellar »Treasure Chamber«. In the barrels, top wines are stored to ennoble first class harvests

66

Port wine is not only a question of taste and profitable trade good. Deep in its chambers, the state »Instituto do Vinho do Porto« watches over these oldest remaining bottles like museum specimens

Testing and tasting the wines in the port wine institute is
a delicate task. The tasting is done from commercial
producers' bottles that are rendered unidentifiable, and
ultimately serves to market a particular variety of wine.
The taste test is one of the measures in judging the quality
and is part of a series of exactly defined control tasks.
Among these are collecting all freely available Douro
wines, inspecting the exporters, supervising the following
of the respective production regulations for the various
quality standards, as well as providing certificates of origin

Control activities are complemented by the Technical
Services. They are dedicated to physical-chemical as well
as to microbiological examinations; they also conduct
studies to optimize wine growing and storage technology
and basic agricultural research. The business services of
the »Instituto do Vinho do Porto«, founded in 1933 and
bestowed with extended competences in 1936, include
working out market strategies and media presentation
independent of individual companies, to secure and
improve the worldwide sales prospects of the product
»port wine«

69

The »Vinho do Porto« is traditionally served in a »Cálice«.
In 1790, a Scot named George Sandeman founded his port
wine company, today one of the most reputed of the
world-famous producers. The »Don« is the trademark
introduced in 1928: with his cape, the black »Capa«, and
with the broad-rimmed hat, he depicts a student from
Coimbra in the clothing one can still meet him in on festive
occasions there today

70

In every port wine cellarage, private quality controls
independent of the state Port Wine Institute are carried
out. The cellar master takes a sample of a wine that has
already been aging for years. The taste test as well as the
laboratory analysis are to determine whether the wine and
the barrel's wood have survived the long time period
without damage. Along with the aging in barrels, some
wine ages in bottles

Wine growing in the Alto Douro stretches along the
mountain ridges and down into the shore areas of the Rio
Douro and can claim a tradition of thousands of years.
After 1703, the British profited greatly from wine exporting
because of an unfair trade agreement with the Portuguese.
In the 18th century, the legendary Marquês de Pombal
instituted in this region the world's first bounded wine
growing territory with legal quality norms. This made it
possible for the »wine from Lamego« or the »Vinho dos
Nobres« (wine for the nobility) – the precursing names for
port wine – to establish themselves as steady export
articles of consistent quality

Wine terraces dominate the landscape. The granite formations exhibit the unfavorable structure peculiar to this location. The rock must be shattered with explosives, so that the vines can take root. The stony ground holds water and releases the day's warmth to the plants during the night, contributing to the characteristic rounded-out taste of the grapes grown in the Alto Douro. The climatic conditions alternate, with an extremely hot late summer and cold winters. From Barca d'Alva in the east, on the Spanish border, the railway line »Linha do Douro« stretches through the picturesque vineyard landscape along the river to the »Estação de São Bento« in Porto

Ponte Dona Maria Pia, constructed by Gustave Eiffel (1877)

*Below the car bridge Ponte da Arrábida, the warehouses
recall Porto's former function as a river port*

The mighty iron construction of the Ponte D.Luís I is an
eye-catching spectacle. At a height of 60 meters, the upper
traffic lane runs 172 meters across the river. The lower
lane connects the shores at a height of 10 meters. The
construction, finished in 1866, replaced a suspension
bridge whose two remaining pylons seem as small as toys
beside the gateway of the Ponte D.Luís I

The many filigree iron constructions determine the city's appearance in general and in detail. Railings, portals, window bars, and the innumerable balconies testify to highly specialized art metalworkers. This part of the city's architecture is increasingly being forgotten, replaced by modern constructions of dubious esthetics – perhaps this portal roofing of a former tobacco factory will survive all modernization plans

The iron-glass construction of the former »Mercado da Fruta« – the market hall »Mercado Ferreira Borges« – serves today as a stylish art forum for changing exhibits

*The »Casa de Serralves«, with its varying exhibits and its
wonderful botanical gardens is a happy symbiosis of art
and nature*

A view over the inner city toward Praça da Liberdade.
The little green islands disappear in the sea of buildings

80

In the landscape of densely interlocked red roofs, the glass clear skylights capture daylight for the stairwells

The skylights glow like buoys – the »Clara Bóias«. In regard to the number and variety of these iron and glass constructions, Porto is unique in the world. From the street, it's not always possible to spot these islands of light, sometimes reminiscent of little greenhouses, making their own contribution to the art of building, or simply capping the roof with a playful ornament

82

Porto is a city of churches. In an outer district, the inconspicuous Gothic-style »Mosteiro de Leça do Balio« has been witness to more than 500 years of history. It serves as a motif for developing artists, as does the Sé Cathedral from the 12th and 13th centuries. The twisted »Pelourinho« column announces the city's rights. In the 9th century, the officially documented »cradle of the city« stood here in the area of today's »Bairro da Sé«

The Sé Cathedral: Sedes Episcopales – the Bishop's seat

*The mysterious catacombs of the Igreja de São Francisco
from the 14th and 15th centuries served as a cemetery in
the first half of the 19th century. The deceased were buried
not only in the masonry, but also under the wood planks
of the floor. In the underground cemetery, difficult of
access, old plaques commemorate the last resting place of
members and patrons of the Franciscan Order*

86

The »Sacristia« of the Igreja das Carmelitas, from the 17th century, is held in heavy rare wood. The dark ceiling painting survived – as undamaged as the artistic interior – through the confused years of a historical epoch in which the sacristy was used by the military as a stable for horses. Porto's pompous church buildings and life's solid embeddedness in Catholicism have long been combined with the inhabitants' will to social reform and political liberalism

The »Arabian Salon« of 1880 is one of Europe's unique
works of architecture and is located among other
impressive halls in the »Palácio da Bolsa« – the »Palace of
the Bourse«, the seat of the influential trade association
of Porto. Today, the artistically decorated »Salão Arabe« is
used as an auditorium for receptions and concerts

The »Coliseu« is used as a multi-purpose stage.
Advertisements are affixed to the hanging curtain. Films
alternate with the most various live shows – from the
circus to solo performances to rock concerts. The building
from the 1930's stands under Monument Preservation

All too often, the »inner life« escapes unnoticed. Behind heavy façades, people live and work in an elegant ambience that awakens memories of European metropoles in long-vanished times. The publisher's bookstore »Lello & Irmão« offers contemporary literature in a historical costume

*The bookstore »Lello«
has always been in family
hands*

The »Escritórios« have, by now, become unique in Europe.
In the business offices of the old port city, sleeve protectors
are no rarity, even though computers have long since
invaded these offices, too, with their standing desks and
old wooden interiors

Office in a trading company: the generations-old furniture still serves its purpose

93

A long »Eléctrico« ride leads out of the historic city district
»Barredo«, with its authentic charm and pure urbanity, and
out along curvy shore road that hugs the Rio Douro. Riding
by, many buildings awaken memories of those times
when the river still served as a port. At »Foz do Douro«,
the streetcar bends away along the Atlantic, leading as
far as the industrial suburb Matosinhos

94

Trading ships no longer dock on the quays of the »Ribeira«

95

The mouth of the Rio Douro opens wide into the Atlantic.
The traffic lane of the highway bridge Ponte da Arrábida
(1963) is suspended across the river valley with a length of
500 meters

The ocean crashes at »Foz«. The Avenida do Brazil divides the row of buildings from the beach, the promenades, and the cafés

*Canneries dominate life in Matosinhos. For some time
now, economic growth has been dynamic around Porto,
influencing this northern suburb as well. Many investors
from the Common Market grasp the opportunity to
locate their production sites in the greater Porto area.
Matosinhos blends into Leixões – Porto's true port*

98

In the area of the river's mouth, one can expect fog banks that quickly drift into the city. Then, in the still-sunny inner city, one can hear the foghorns blowing from afar. The mouth – »Foz do Douro« – is also the name of this district, and »Foz Velha« is a preferred place to live. It exhibits a mixture of simple little village-like houses and exclusive new buildings

Sea resorts like Miramar or Granja lie on the railway line.
The beautiful beaches stretch for dozens of kilometers
past Espinho far into the south. »Barracas«, reminiscent
of Saracen tents, offer shelter from sun and wind. In the
evenings, the tarpaulins are removed from the frames.
The chapel »Senhor da Pedra« greets the ships going to sea
from Porto or calling at this old and honorable trading
and port city from all over the world

Porto has relocated its port to Leixões, to the north outside
its gates. Not far away, airplanes land and take off from the
airport »Pedras Rubras«. The region is increasingly one of
Europe's important economic regions. An expressway
connects the inner city with Leixões. Here is a bustling
maritime confusion of trading ships, sport boats, and sport
yachts fit for the open seas. Beginners are taught the
secrets of seafaring in a separate part of the port facilities

On the »Cais da Ribeira«:
Life, noise, smells – and,
in the dark, arched
passageways, many a
hidden little restaurant
with excellent cuisine

The so-called Rua Escura: in the depths of this weft of alleys, the market unfolds itself with an almost Asiatic atmosphere

Old advertisements remind one of long-vanished colonial times

*A neighborly chat across the street below in »Miragaia«.
Like the »Ribeira«, this is a district with houses crowded
against each other and is among the most densely
populated parts of the big city*

105

*What would Porto be without its festivals! – from Carnival
through St.John's Night to the Church and secular
holidays. Music is always a part of things – sometimes
played by the »Bombeiros Voluntários« – the »Voluntary
Fire Department« – sometimes performed by the school
bands, always in uniform*

The city extends ever further beyond its administrative boundaries. But the villages in the nearer metropolitan area keep their traditions alive. In the autumn, the »Desfolhada« is celebrated – the harvest and shucking of the maize, accompanied by the jolly spontaneous antiphonal songs »Cantar à desgarrada«

107

Fruit, vegetables, field crops, or cabbage for the »Caldo Verde« soup: Moving street shops create a changing city scene. All the products are from the immediate surroundings. The fishermen live in the little village Afurada on the other side of the mouth of the Rio Douro

108

Fresh-caught fish. The vendors are often fishermen's wives. Mussels and the most various crustaceans from crayfish to large prawns are also available

109

*Troublesome patching of
the finely woven net*

In the cooler season, it is often moist. Then it is very difficult to dry the laundry. Every ray of sun is used

111

The Atlantic rolls right up to the gates of the city – with storms and high seas in the winter, sometimes causing sailing disasters. There are even some wrecks rotting on the ocean floor. In front of the »Forte de São Francisco Xavier« with the popular nickname »Castelo do Queijo« (cheese castle – because of its strange rock formations), the bow of a burst and burnt-out tanker bears witness to such an accident. The numerous sport fishermen can be seen in every kind of weather

The sand bank in the Rio Douro is considered an ideal fishing spot

With its height of 75 meters, the baroque Igreja e Torre dos Clérigos, built by the Italian architect Niccolò Nasoni, has been an unmistakable landmark since the 18th century

Graphic shadow patterns of the promenades on the Atlantic

Old warehouse, depots, and customs houses testify to
Porto's former importance as a port city on the river. Old
engravings and paintings, but also photos from not all too
distant days, show the Rio Douro full of ships. The
functional shift of the city from the transhipping of goods
to a center of industry and trade proceeds apace

Views of the river mirror the many-faceted image of the city. In harmony with the cathedral, the Bishop's seat at Porto's historical birthplace dominates the ancient quarter »Ribeira«, with its market stands, its simple housing, its sprinkling of tourist restaurants, and the very lively activity of its inhabitants

In the restless, pulsing bustle of the inner city, time sometimes seems to stand still

View from Vila Nova de Gaia. The Rio Douro flows past the
»Ribeira« district toward the Atlantic. The river has been a
determining factor in the long and changing development
of the former »Portus Cale«, which history has given the
title of an invincible city: »Porto – Cidade Invicta«

Photo credits

Werner Radasewsky
*10, 16 (2 photos), 18, 19, 20, 21, 22 (bottom), 23, 24, 25,
27, 28, 30, 31, 32, 33, 38, 40, 41, 42, 43, 44, 45, 46, 47, 60
(bottom), 61 (2 photos), 62 (3 photos), 63 (3 photos), 64, 65,
72, 73, 74, 75, 76, 77, 78, 79, 80, 81, 82, 83 (3 photos), 84
(2 photos), 85, 94, 95, 96, 97, 98, 99, 100, 102, 103, 104, 105,
106, 107, 109, 110, 111, 112 (2 photos), 113, 114, 115, 116, 118,
119, Back Cover (Dust Jacket)*

Günter Schneider
*Cover (Dust Jacket), 2/3, 6/7, 8/9, 17, 22 (top), 29, 34, 35,
36, 37, 39, 48, 49, 50, 51, 52, 53, 54, 55, 56, 57, 58, 59, 60
(top), 66, 67, 68, 69, 70, 71, 86, 87, 88, 89, 90, 91, 92, 93, 101,
108, 117*

The photo on pages 4/5 was taken by Manfred Hamm.